DKfindout!

Energy

Author: Emily Dodd
Consultant: Jack Challoner

D0177205

DK | Penguin Random House

Editors Olivia Stanford, Abhijit Dutta,
Kritika Gupta
Project art editor Hoa Luc
Art editors Roohi Rais,
Shubham Rohatgi
Senior art editor Nidhi Mehra
DTP designers Dheeraj Singh,
Rajesh Singh Adhikari
Picture researcher Nishwan Rasool
Jacket co-ordinator Francesca Young
Jacket designer Dheeraj Arora
Managing editors Laura Gilbert,
Monica Saigal
Managing art editor Diane Peyton Jones
Deputy managing art editor Ivy Sengupta
Senior pre-production producer Tony Phipps
Pre-production producer Rob Dunn
Senior producer Isabell Schart
Creative director Helen Senior
Publishing director Sarah Larter

Educational consultant Jacqueline Harris

First published in Great Britain in 2018 by
Dorling Kindersley Limited
80 Strand, London, WC2R 0RL

Copyright © 2018 Dorling Kindersley Limited
A Penguin Random House Company
10 9 8 7 6 5 4 3 2 1
001–308820–July/2018

A CIP catalogue record for this book
is available from the British Library.
ISBN: 978-0-2413-2301-4

Printed and bound in China

A WORLD OF IDEAS:
SEE ALL THERE IS TO KNOW

www.dk.com

Contents

Coal fire

Racing car

Ice cubes

2

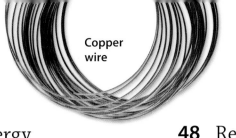
Copper wire

Inside the Earth

Voltaic pile

Rocket take off

What is energy?

Energy makes everything happen. All moving objects have energy, but light, heat, magnetism, and electricity are types of energy, too. Energy can change from one form to another, such as electrical energy becoming light energy in a lamp, or it can be stored ready to use later, like the energy in a battery.

Indestructible energy

Energy cannot be created or destroyed, it just changes from one type of energy to another. This is called the conservation of energy.

Light energy
Light energy from the Sun travels to Earth and some of it is taken in by the leaves of plants.

Begin with a bang

Scientists have found evidence that a massive explosion, 13.8 billion years ago, made all the energy that exists in the Universe. This giant explosion that created time and space is known as the Big Bang.

A world of energy
We use energy all the time to power our homes, schools, and work places. The light energy we use at night is so bright it can be seen from space.

Chemical energy
A plant uses light energy to make food. It stores this food as sugar. Sugar contains chemical energy.

Chemical energy
When we eat plants our bodies either break down this food to use right away, or store it as chemical energy.

Movement energy
Our bodies change stored energy to movement energy. Energy also helps us to grow and keep warm.

The Sun

The main source of energy for planet Earth is our closest star, the Sun. This ball of glowing gas gives us heat to keep warm and light to see. Heat and light also drive our weather systems, and provide energy for plants to grow.

Superhot
The surface of the Sun is 5,500°C (10,000°F), but its core is 15 million °C (27 million °F).

Energy inside the Earth

We get some of our energy from inside the Earth. Below the surface is a hot layer called the mantle. Below that is an even hotter core. The heat rises to the surface where it causes the movement of rocks, and powers volcanoes and earthquakes.

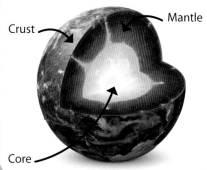

Crust

Mantle

Core

Energy and atoms

Atoms are the tiny particles everything is made from. Inside every atom there are even smaller particles, which are held together by invisible forces that store energy.

Inside an atom

Atoms are made of three different types of particle – positively charged protons, negatively charged electrons, and neutrons, which have no charge. Protons and neutrons are found in the centre of the atom, in its nucleus.

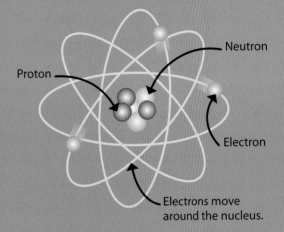

Neutron

Proton

Electron

Electrons move around the nucleus.

Energy from atoms

The Sun is mostly made of hydrogen gas. It is so hot that its atoms lose their electrons, so just the nucleus remains. In the Sun, hydrogen nuclei join, or fuse, to make nuclei of helium atoms. This process, called nuclear fusion, releases lots of energy.

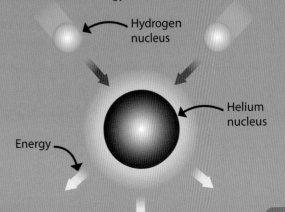

Hydrogen nucleus

Helium nucleus

Energy

Giant loop

The Sun's superhot gases can form huge loops. If they break, these loops can send out high-energy matter into space. This matter can interrupt radio and television broadcasts on Earth, 150 million km (93 million miles) away.

Types of energy

Energy is all around us! Without it, nothing could happen. Sometimes, energy is obvious to us, such as the heat energy we feel from a warm drink. However, we are often not aware of it at all. There are many different kinds of energy – here are some of them.

Heat

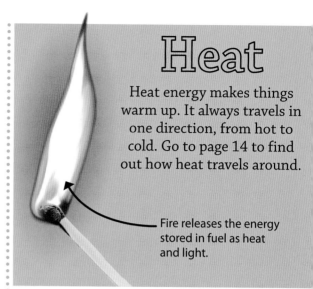

Heat energy makes things warm up. It always travels in one direction, from hot to cold. Go to page 14 to find out how heat travels around.

Fire releases the energy stored in fuel as heat and light.

Potential

Potential energy is stored in objects that are ready to do something. When we pull back the string of a bow, we store energy in the string, ready to fire the arrow. Turn to page 10 to find out more about the types of potential energy.

Kinetic

Anything in the Universe that is moving has kinetic energy. Kinetic energy is another name for movement energy. Go to page 12 to see kinetic energy in action.

LIGHT

Glowing objects give out light energy. This energy travels in straight lines, and bounces off objects and into our eyes so we can see them. Turn to page 18 to learn more about light.

Chemical

Chemical energy is stored in the bonds that hold atoms together in chemicals. We break down the bonds in chemicals in our food to release this energy. Go to page 28 to uncover more about chemical energy.

SOUND

Sound energy is produced when objects vibrate. We can hear a guitar because vibrations travel from the strings, through the air, to our ears. Go to page 22 to discover more about sound energy.

NUCLEAR

Nuclear energy is stored inside atoms. The energy is released when atoms are split apart or join together. Go to page 26 to see how we use nuclear energy.

ELECTRICAL

When charged particles build up or move together they have electrical energy. A flow of charged particles creates a current, which we can use to power appliances. Go to page 36 to explore electricity.

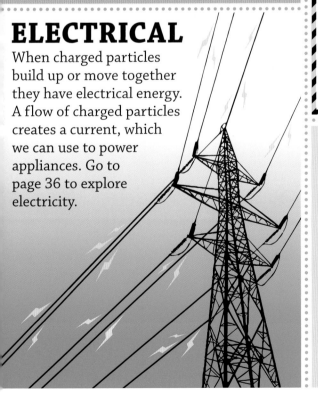

Magnetic

Magnets store magnetic energy in an invisible force field. This field causes a push or pull on other magnets or magnetic objects. Go to page 34 to investigate magnetic energy.

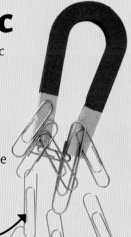

Steel paperclips are magnetic.

Potential energy

Any type of energy that is stored and ready to do something is called potential energy. Potential energy is found inside everything from chemicals and elastic to electricity and everyday objects. If you ride a bike to the top of a hill, its potential energy increases. The bike is then ready to roll down the other side.

Elastic potential energy

This energy is stored in a material when you stretch or squash it. Once stretched, the material is ready to spring back. Elastic potential energy is also called spring energy, for this reason!

The bow string is stretched and ready to spring back to fire the arrow.

How springs work

A spring can be made from any firm and flexible material, wound around in circles. The material and shape let the spring store elastic potential energy. Some mattresses contain springs, which make you bounce if you jump on the bed!

A metal spring

Gravitational potential energy

All objects on the Earth's surface have the force of gravity pulling them downwards. This gives them gravitational potential energy. The higher an object is, and the heavier it is, the more gravitational potential energy it has.

The gravitational potential energy of the weight is increased when it is lifted up.

! WOW!

Fleas store **elastic potential energy** in their legs, which allows them to jump **130 times** their body length.

Kinetic energy

Anything that moves has kinetic energy. This can be passed on between objects. When you kick a ball, the energy from your foot gives the ball energy to move. Most kinetic energy ends up as heat energy. You can turn movement into heat by rubbing your hands together!

Movement energy
Another name for kinetic energy is movement energy. When an animal, such as a cheetah, runs, it changes the potential chemical energy stored in its muscles into kinetic energy.

! WOW!

The cheetah is the **fastest land animal**. It can run at **112 kph (70 mph)**.

The faster the cheetah runs, the more kinetic energy it has. Every time it doubles its speed, the amount of energy it has is quadrupled.

Energy and forces

A force is a push or pull. When forces move objects, they change the amount or type of energy they have. Gravity is a force that pulls everything down towards the Earth's surface. This force changes the potential energy of a pencil in your hand to kinetic energy when you drop it.

The push force of throwing a ball gives the ball kinetic energy.

Heat

Hot things have more energy than cold things. Boiling hot water, for example, has much more energy than cold water. This energy always moves from hot to cold, and we call it heat. Heat travels in three different ways: conduction, convection, and radiation.

Conduction

Conduction is how heat travels through an object, or between objects when they touch. If your hand is cold and you hold hands with someone with a warm hand, their heat energy travels into your hand and it feels warm.

Heat energy travels along the hot metal rod from the warmer end to the cooler one.

Fire

Discovery of fire

When humans were able to start and control fires, it changed the way they lived. They could use the energy released from burning wood to keep warm, cook food, and scare away dangerous animals.

Convection

When a liquid or gas is heated up it expands and floats upwards. This is called convection. If the fluid cools, it sinks back down again. This creates a circular flow of movement called a convection current.

The water at the bottom of the pan warms and moves upwards, carrying the peas with it.

We can feel the heat from a fire without touching it because of radiation.

Radiation

Hot things produce invisible rays called infrared radiation. When these rays hit objects, they warm them. We feel warmth from the Sun because of these rays. It only takes eight minutes for radiated heat to reach us from the Sun.

Hot and cold

The temperature of an object depends on how the particles that make it up move around. If we add heat energy to a solid, its particles begin to move and it melts into a liquid. If we add more heat energy, the particles move even faster and the liquid evaporates into a gas.

Melting and boiling points

Different materials have different melting and boiling points. These are the temperatures at which a solid changes into a liquid, and then a gas. These processes can also work in reverse.

Solid
Solid water is called ice. The particles in a solid are in fixed positions. They vibrate, but they don't move around – this is why solids keep their shape.

FREEZING

DEPOSITION

SUBLIMATION

BOILING

Water vapour can turn straight into a solid by a process called deposition.

Solids can change straight into gases in a process called sublimation.

Gas
Water as a gas is called water vapour. Particles in a gas move quickly away from each other in all directions, filling the space they are in. When invisible water vapour starts to cool, it makes tiny droplets of liquid, which create steam.

Absolute zero

Lord Kelvin

William Thomson, also called Lord Kelvin, was a scientist who worked out that if we took all the heat energy away from an object, so its particles couldn't move, its temperature would be –273°C (–460°F). This is known as absolute zero.

Below 0°C (32°F), water freezes to become ice.

Above 0°C (32°F), the particles in ice start to slide past each other and it melts to become liquid water.

MELTING

CONDENSING

Liquid
Particles in a liquid can move past each other. This is why water takes the shape of the container it is in.

Above 100°C (212°F), water boils as its particles escape their container. The liquid evaporates into a gas.

If water vapour drops below 100°C (212°F), it condenses to form liquid water.

Temperature

Temperature is a measure of how hot or cold something is. We can measure temperature using a thermometer. We usually measure temperature in degrees Celsius (°C) or degrees Fahrenheit (°F).

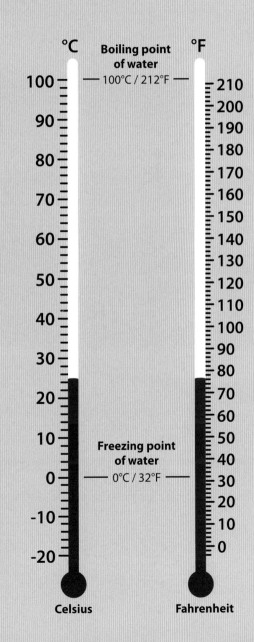

°C

Boiling point of water
— 100°C / 212°F —

°F

100
90
80
70
60
50
40
30
20
10
0
-10
-20

Freezing point of water
— 0°C / 32°F —

210
200
190
180
170
160
150
140
130
120
110
100
90
80
70
60
50
40
30
20
10
0

Celsius

Fahrenheit

Light

Light is the type of energy that allows us to see. Glowing things give off light, which travels in straight lines. All the colours we see are types of light called "visible light". When this light bounces off objects into our eyes we see them – a flower looks red because it reflects red light.

The light bends and slows down as it enters the solid prism. Each colour bends a different amount.

A beam of white light enters the prism.

Splitting light
White light contains different colours! It can be separated into all the colours it contains using a triangular-shaped block of glass called a prism.

Glow in the dark

Some animals use chemical energy to create their own light. This is called bioluminescence. Other animals can use their bodies like a prism and split white light into its different colours.

Ctenophores, also called comb jellies, split white light with their hairy, comb-like fins.

Shadows

Shadows are areas of darkness where light has been blocked by an object. They take the shape of the object that is in the way because light travels in straight lines. Objects that block light completely are described as opaque.

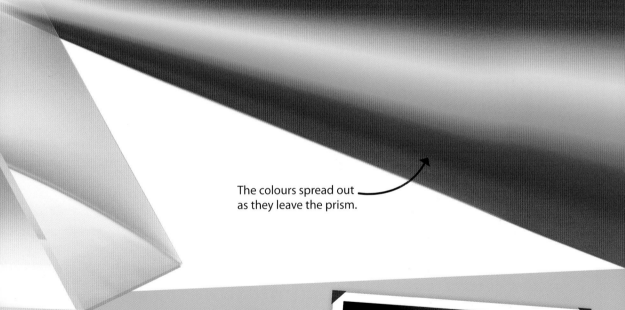

The colours spread out as they leave the prism.

Some tiny ocean life forms called algae flash using glowing chemicals, to warn predators away.

A firefly uses a chemical reaction in its body to create light to attract a mate.

Invisible rays

The light we see makes up a tiny part of the energy that comes from the Sun. Beams of visible light and invisible rays make up something called the electromagnetic spectrum. Both are made of particles, called photons, and travel in waves. The photons of different rays have different amounts of energy. We can only detect these rays using special instruments.

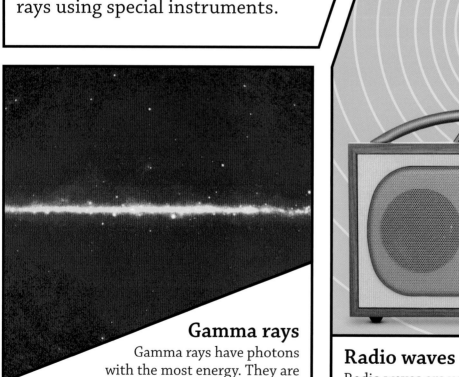

Gamma rays

Gamma rays have photons with the most energy. They are dangerous rays that are made by nuclear explosions and radioactive materials. They also come from exploding stars! This picture shows gamma rays from space in orange.

Radio waves

Radio waves are used to carry signals. We use them to transmit television and radio programmes, which are picked up by appliances that change the signals into sound and pictures.

Ultraviolet

Ultraviolet light, or UV, can be seen by some animals, including bees. Flowers have markings that reflect UV light, which attract insects and guide them to land, just like lights on an airport runway.

Microwaves

Microwaves can be used to heat up food. They vibrate the water, fat, and sugar particles in the food, and as the particles wobble they heat up. You need to stir the food to spread the heat around evenly.

Ping!

X-rays

X-rays have lots of energy. They travel through soft materials, such as skin, but bounce off hard objects, such as bones. We can shine X-rays through people to take a picture of their skeleton.

Infrared

Warm objects give out rays called infrared radiation. There are infrared rays beaming away from your body right now! Special cameras can detect infrared and create a picture, where hotter areas are yellow and colder areas are purple.

Woof! Woof!

Sound

Sounds are made when something vibrates, changing movement energy into sound energy. Sound travels through solids, liquids, and gases as waves. The waves are caused by the vibrations, which make particles knock into each other. Sound cannot travel in space because there are no air particles for it to travel through.

The particles spread out after being squashed.

The vibrations squash particles together.

Sound waves

Sound travels in waves that first squash particles together, then spread them out. It's a ripple of energy that spreads out from its source. When a wolf howls, folds inside its throat vibrate, sending sound waves through the air.

Decibels

We measure the energy of a sound in decibels. Here are some familiar sounds with their volume in decibels.

Human whisper across room	Acoustic guitar 1 m (3 ft) away	Car 1 m (3 ft) away	By speakers at a concert

| 10 | 20 | 30 | 40 | 50 | 60 | 70 | 80 | 90 | 100 | 11 |

Echoes

Echoes happen when a sound wave bounces off something and comes back. Echoes don't take long to return, as sound travels quickly.

Rocky surfaces reflect sound well, producing clear echoes.

Pitch

The faster something vibrates, the higher the sound it makes. Slower vibrations make lower sounds. Pitch is the word we use to describe how high or low a sound is.

Sound waves changing with pitch

High pitch

Low pitch

Covering different holes on a recorder changes the pitch of the sound.

Volume

The bigger the vibration of something, the more energy it has and the louder the volume of the sound produced. Smaller vibrations make quieter sounds.

Sound waves changing with volume

Loud

Quiet

Sound waves spread out as they travel further from their source.

As the energy of the waves is spread over a larger area they sound quieter.

Lion's roar next to you

Jet engine close by

Explosion close by

20   130   140   150

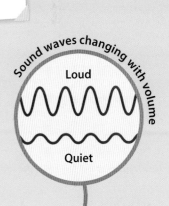

Super sound

Sound energy travels through air at a speed of around 340 m (1,120 ft) per second. This speed is also known as Mach 1. If something travels faster than Mach 1, we say it is supersonic – that means it is travelling faster than sound.

When an aircraft gets near supersonic speeds, the particles of air behind it spread out, which lowers the temperature.

Sonic boom
When an aircraft travels at the speed of sound, it creates a big noise called a sonic boom. It is made because the plane catches up with its own sound waves, squashing them together. Travelling at speeds near Mach 1 can also create a cone-shaped cloud called a vapour cone.

The cone-shaped cloud is made of droplets of water that have condensed out of the air as the temperature fell.

Infrasound

The slower something vibrates, the lower the pitch of the sound it makes. Infrasound is sound that is too low for humans to hear. However some animals, such as elephants and whales, can make and hear these super-low noises.

Elephants use infrasound to communicate with each other.

The vapour cone will disappear as the air returns to normal.

Seeing with sound

Sound pulses travel through air or water, bounce off objects, and come back to us as echoes. We can time these echoes to work out how far away objects are.

A submarine uses sonar to help it avoid obstacles such as icebergs.

Sonar
Ships and submarines use sonar machines to send out sound pulses. They use the echoes to detect ships and other objects in their path.

Dolphins make high-pitched clicks to help them find fish.

Echolocation
Some animals, including bats and dolphins, send out pulses of sound to help them track down their prey. Using sound in this way is called echolocation.

Nuclear energy

All matter is made of atoms. Atoms contain particles called protons and neutrons, which are held together by a nuclear force – a bit like magnetism, but much, much stronger. When these particles are divided, energy is released. We can split atoms apart in a nuclear power station, to release energy to make electricity.

5

3

7

Radioactive waste

The materials used in nuclear power stations are radioactive substances. These materials, including uranium, give out harmful rays. They must be disposed of carefully, as they are dangerous for the environment.

Nuclear waste is harmful.

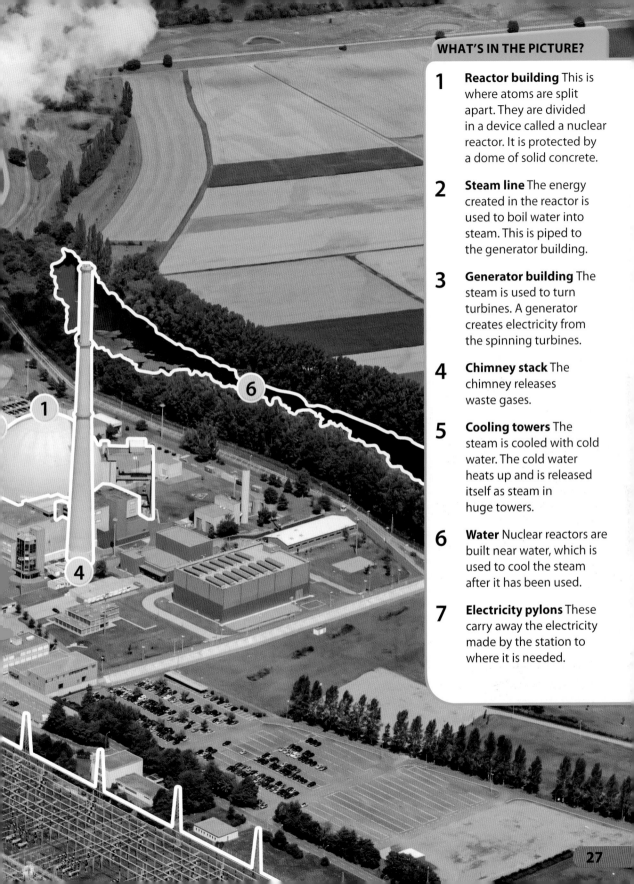

WHAT'S IN THE PICTURE?

1 Reactor building This is where atoms are split apart. They are divided in a device called a nuclear reactor. It is protected by a dome of solid concrete.

2 Steam line The energy created in the reactor is used to boil water into steam. This is piped to the generator building.

3 Generator building The steam is used to turn turbines. A generator creates electricity from the spinning turbines.

4 Chimney stack The chimney releases waste gases.

5 Cooling towers The steam is cooled with cold water. The cold water heats up and is released itself as steam in huge towers.

6 Water Nuclear reactors are built near water, which is used to cool the steam after it has been used.

7 Electricity pylons These carry away the electricity made by the station to where it is needed.

Chemical energy

There is energy stored inside all substances in their chemical bonds. These are the forces that hold atoms together. The chemical name for water is H_2O because it is made of two hydrogen atoms and one oxygen atom, joined together with chemical bonds. Energy is released when new bonds are made during chemical reactions.

Potassium iodide is a catalyst.

Mix of hydrogen peroxide, food colouring, and washing-up liquid.

The washing-up liquid and oxygen bubbles make foam.

1

2

Elephant's toothpaste
In this reaction, a chemical called hydrogen peroxide breaks down into water and oxygen. This happens naturally, but potassium iodide is added as a catalyst. Catalysts make chemical reactions happen faster.

Chemical reaction
The hydrogen peroxide breaks apart to form oxygen and water. The oxygen gas bubbles out into the washing-up liquid to make foam. The formation of oxygen gas also produces heat.

Activation energy

Some chemical reactions need energy to start them off. The heat energy made when striking a match starts a reaction in the chemicals in the match tip and the surface of the box that produces a flame.

The friction of striking a match provides the activation energy to make a flame.

Everyday reactions

Chemical reactions can release lots of energy when chemicals bubble or explode, but there are much slower, less noticeable chemical reactions happening all around us.

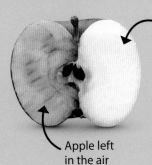

Freshly cut apple

Brown apple
The inside of a freshly cut apple reacts with oxygen in the air in a chemical reaction that makes the flesh turn brown.

Apple left in the air

Rusting nail
Iron and steel slowly react with water and oxygen in the air to form a new substance, called rust.

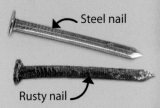

Steel nail

Rusty nail

The foam expands and moves out of the glass.

3

The colourless part of the egg turns white when it is cooked.

Forming foam
The energy released during the reaction produces lots of heat and the movement of the oxygen. The large amount of foam spills out of the glass like toothpaste, which gives the reaction its name.

Frying an egg
When you heat up an egg, the proteins inside it react and join up with each other. The joined-up proteins make the egg turn white.

Explosions

Explosions are quick releases of lots of energy. They are often loud, bright, and very hot. Fireworks go off when chemicals react together, releasing bursts of light and sound. Volcanoes erupt when pressure builds up underground and is suddenly released, spraying out rock and lava.

Under pressure

Pressure is the name we give to the pushing force of something that is being squashed and contained. When you pump up a bike tyre you squash more air in, increasing the pressure. If you add too much the tyre will burst! Many explosions are caused by pressure building up.

Lava is thrown out of erupting volcanoes.

Volcanoes
When pressure builds up in the liquid rock beneath the Earth's surface, it can explode out in a volcanic eruption. Volcanoes can be so powerful that they turn rock into dust, called ash!

Chemical explosion

When a firework is lit it gives the chemicals inside it enough energy to start reacting. The reactions produce lots of gas, and that gas increases the pressure, making the firework explode. The reactions also release light, sound, and heat. Different chemicals make the explosion different colours.

Bubbles of gas violently push the soda out of the bottle.

Eruption of a hot-water geyser

Soda explosion

If you drop a mint into a fizzy drink, the carbon dioxide dissolved in the drink starts to bubble out as gas – creating a soda explosion!

Geysers

Hot rocks underground can heat water until it boils. This increases the pressure, and water and steam can explode outwards as a geyser.

Energy from food

Wave your hand – the energy you used to wave came from your food. Food contains stored chemical energy. Your body breaks your food down into simple chemicals that can be stored for later, or used to help you move and keep warm.

Carbohydrate
Bread, pasta, and potatoes contain carbohydrates. They contain lots of energy that is released slowly by our bodies. A slice of bread contains about 70 calories.

Calories
The energy inside food is measured in calories. We can use these measurements to compare the energy in different foods. However, food doesn't just provide us with energy. It also gives us important nutrients, so it is important to eat a balanced diet.

Protein
Meat, fish, eggs, and nuts contain protein. Protein is used to grow and repair parts of the body. A cooked chicken leg has around 150 calories.

Fibre
Fruit and vegetables are important because they contain fibre, vitamins, and minerals. Fibre helps our digestion, but it is low in energy. A serving of broccoli contains about 10 calories.

Sugar
Sugar quickly releases energy to our bodies. Too much sugar is bad for us because the body can't use it, so converts it to fat. A scoop of ice cream has about 130 calories.

Storing energy

Animals store extra energy as fat. This is useful for animals that have access to lots of food for a short time, but that need to go without food for long periods. A thick layer of fat can also help to keep animals warm.

A walrus has a layer of fat, called blubber, that helps to keep it warm.

Fat

Eating fat gives us lots of energy. We need to exercise to burn off the energy that eating fat gives us. A slice of pizza contains about 185 calories.

Plant power

Plants make their own food in a process called photosynthesis. They use carbon dioxide gas from the air, water from the ground, and the Sun's light energy to create sugars.

Sunlight
Light energy from the Sun is changed into stored chemical energy in the plant.

Leaf
Leaves contain a chemical called chlorophyll. This helps the plant take in the energy of sunlight.

Oxygen
Plants make oxygen during photosynthesis.

Carbon dioxide
Plants take in carbon dioxide from the air through tiny holes in the leaf.

Stem
Sugars are moved around the plant through its stem.

Roots
Roots anchor the plant and take in water and minerals from the ground.

Water
Water is taken from the roots to the leaves.

Magnetism

Magnets have an invisible force field of energy around them called a magnetic field. This field can push away magnetic objects or pull them near. It may seem like magic, but it is the energy in the magnetic field that gives the magnetic objects the power to move.

Electromagnets

Electricity can make magnets and magnets can make electricity! If electricity is sent through a wire, it creates a magnetic field around it. These types of magnet are called electromagnets. They are useful as they can be turned on or off.

Electromagnetic arm
A powerful electromagnet at the end of this arm is used to separate magnetic from non-magnetic materials. Iron and steel stick to the arm when it is on and are taken to be recycled. To put them down again the magnet is turned off.

Magnetic Earth

Planet Earth is one giant magnet, with a magnetic field that shields us from harmful space rays. A compass works because its metal needle is attracted to the Earth's magnetic field. The marked needle always points north.

The needle of a compass points to magnetic north.

Magnetic objects
Objects that are attracted or repelled by magnetic fields are magnetic. Some metals, including iron, are magnetic. However, most materials, such as wood, plastic, and fabric, are not magnetic.

Electricity

Electrical energy is created by tiny particles that carry electric charge – the most important are electrons. Electrons whizz around atoms, and can jump from one atom to another. An electric current is the movement of trillions of electrons in one direction. Electricity is very useful, but it can also be dangerous!

No electric current
If the electrons in a material are moving around in no particular direction, there is no electric current.

Moving power

Electricity is generated in power stations. This electricity then goes on a journey to reach our homes, schools, and work places. There we can use it to power lights and appliances.

Power stations
Electricity is generated by heating water to make steam. The steam turns a turbine, which makes electricity.

Step-up transformer
A step-up transformer increases the push of the electricity to help travel long distances.

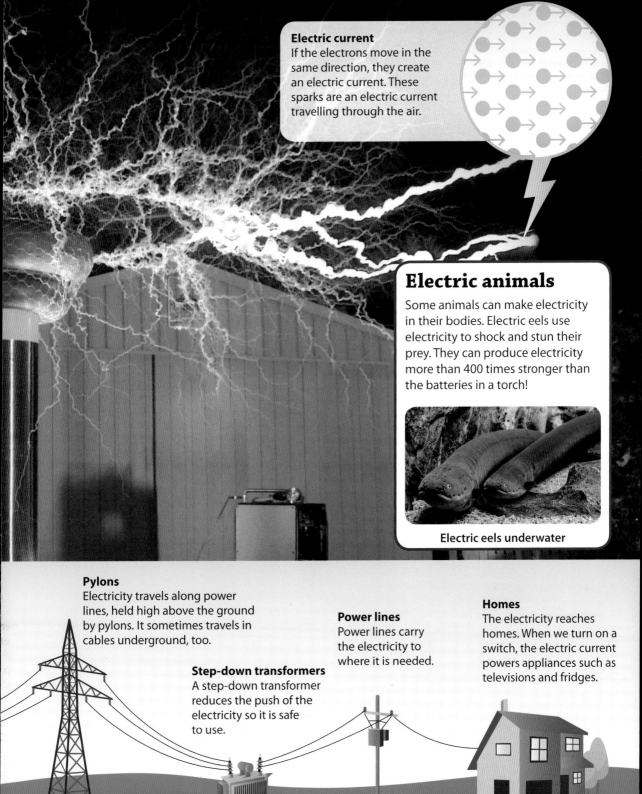

Electric current
If the electrons move in the same direction, they create an electric current. These sparks are an electric current travelling through the air.

Electric animals

Some animals can make electricity in their bodies. Electric eels use electricity to shock and stun their prey. They can produce electricity more than 400 times stronger than the batteries in a torch!

Electric eels underwater

Pylons
Electricity travels along power lines, held high above the ground by pylons. It sometimes travels in cables underground, too.

Step-down transformers
A step-down transformer reduces the push of the electricity so it is safe to use.

Power lines
Power lines carry the electricity to where it is needed.

Homes
The electricity reaches homes. When we turn on a switch, the electric current powers appliances such as televisions and fridges.

Static electricity

When two objects rub together, charged particles can move from one to the other. One object becomes positively charged, the other negatively charged. The build up of charge is called static electricity. Positive and negative charges attract, so the objects stick together!

Electrical attraction
If you rub a balloon on your head, negatively charged electrons from your hair move to the balloon. The balloon becomes negatively charged and pushes away the other electrons in your hair, making the surface of your hair positively charged.

At first, the balloon and the hair have an equal mix of positively and negatively charged particles

Rubbing the balloon against your hair moves electrons from your hair to the balloon.

! **WOW!**

Lightning can be more than five times hotter than the surface of the Sun.

As the balloon gains more negative electrons it becomes negatively charged.

The negatively charged balloon is attracted to positive charges in your hair, so your hair sticks to the balloon.

Lightning

Lightning is a giant spark of electricity. When ice particles in clouds rub together, they can cause charge to build up in the cloud. Eventually, the static electricity becomes so big it jumps between clouds or between the clouds and the Earth as lightning.

Lightning releases heat and light energy.

Circuits

A circuit is a loop that electricity flows through, like water flows through a pipe. This stream of electrical energy is called a current. When you plug in an electrical appliance, such as a games console, and switch it on, you connect it to a circuit.

A switch allows a temporary gap to b made in a circuit so electricity can't flow around it.

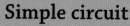

2

1

Simple circuit

A simple circuit has just one loop for electricity to travel around. In this circuit, wires connect the batteries to the light bulbs. Electricity is carried along the wires by electrons, which have an electric charge.

Batteries store chemical energy that can be changed into electrical energy. They have a positive and a negative end.

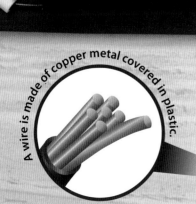

A wire is made of copper metal covered in plastic.

Circuit diagrams

If you want to draw a circuit, you don't have to spend time sketching each bit. Instead, you can use special symbols that represent each part. Can you guess which parts match the symbols below?

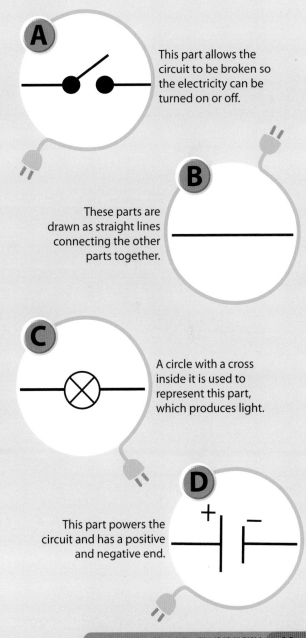

A

This part allows the circuit to be broken so the electricity can be turned on or off.

B

These parts are drawn as straight lines connecting the other parts together.

C

A circle with a cross inside it is used to represent this part, which produces light.

D

This part powers the circuit and has a positive and negative end.

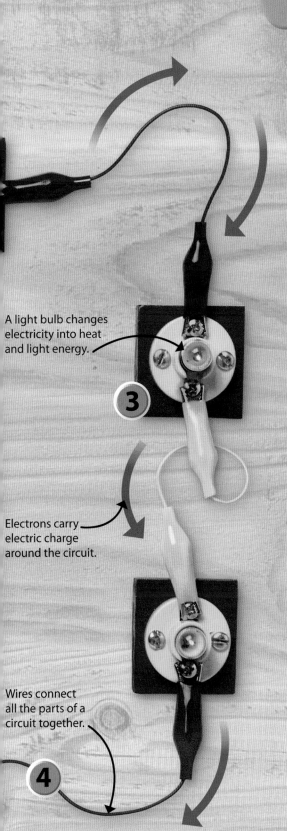

A light bulb changes electricity into heat and light energy.

3

Electrons carry electric charge around the circuit.

Wires connect all the parts of a circuit together.

4

Conductors and insulators

Some materials, such as metals, allow electricity and heat to pass through them easily. We call these conductors. Other materials, such as plastic, don't allow electricity or heat to pass through them easily. They are called insulators. We use conductors and insulators for different jobs.

Glass
Glass doesn't conduct electricity or heat well. It is an insulator, so helps to keep drinks hot or cold.

Which of these are good conductors?

Diamond
Diamond is unusual as it conducts heat well, but it is an insulator of electricity.

Plastic
Plastics are good insulators. Electrical wires often have a plastic coating to keep the electricity inside the wire.

Clothes

Clothes keep us warm as fabric is an insulator. They also trap air near our skin and air is also a good insulator.

Staying warm

A polar bear has insulating fur and a thick layer of fat to help keep it warm. The average winter temperature in the Arctic, where polar bears live, is −29°C (−20°F).

Polar bears live in the freezing Arctic.

Rubber

Rubber is an insulator. It is used in electrical equipment, along with plastics, to stop electricity going where it shouldn't.

Steel

Steel contains iron, which is a metal and a good conductor of heat and electricity.

Graphite

The graphite in pencils is made from carbon, and is a good conductor.

Wood

Wooden spoons can stir hot food without passing the heat from one end of the spoon to the other, so you don't burn your hand!

Making electricity

Whether the energy comes from fossil fuels or renewable technology, nearly all power sources are turned into electricity using turbines and generators. Wind, water, or steam are used to turn a turbine, which makes electricity in a generator using a magnet.

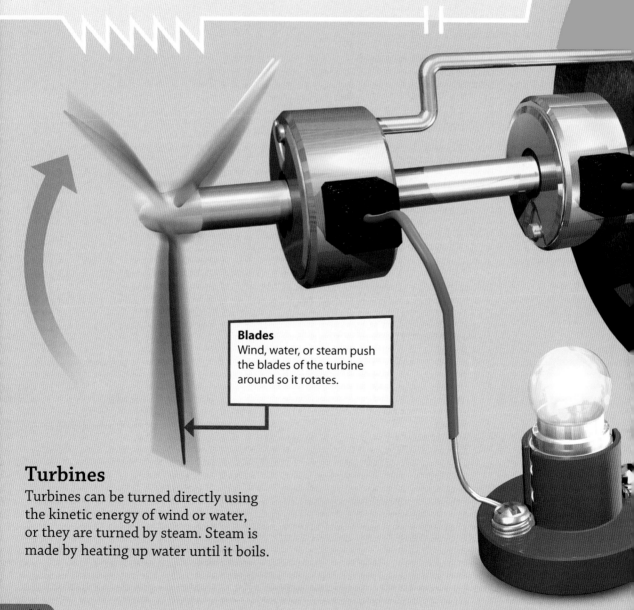

Blades
Wind, water, or steam push the blades of the turbine around so it rotates.

Turbines

Turbines can be turned directly using the kinetic energy of wind or water, or they are turned by steam. Steam is made by heating up water until it boils.

Generators

Turbines are connected to generators. Generators change movement energy into electrical energy using magnets. When a coil of wire is turned in a magnetic field, electricity is made.

The generator is inside the casing behind the turbine.

A wind turbine

Wind turns the blades of the turbine.

Wire
A wire made of copper is turned inside the magnet by the movement of the turbine.

Magnet
The magnet creates a magnetic field. When the wire turns through the magnetic field, electricity flows in the wire.

Electricity
The electricity made by the generator flows around the circuit and into the light bulb.

Charging up

The electrical energy made by a generator can be used immediately, or it can be used to charge a battery. A battery contains chemicals that store electrical energy as chemical energy. Devices such as phones and tablets contain rechargeable batteries.

Portable phone chargers can be used to recharge a phone battery.

Fossil fuels

Coal, oil, and natural gas are fuels that contain a lot of stored energy. We call them fossil fuels. They are made from the remains of fossilized plants and animals that were alive millions of years ago. Fossil fuels burn easily, and release lots of energy as heat when they burn. Their energy is useful for many things, including making electricity in power stations.

Greenhouse gases

The gases in our atmosphere trap some of the heat from the Sun around the Earth, just like a greenhouse. Burning fossil fuels produces carbon dioxide gas, which traps heat. Too much carbon dioxide in the atmosphere causes the planet to warm up.

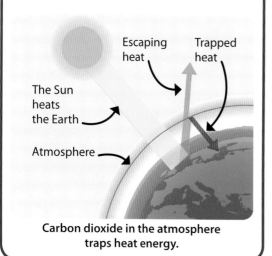

Escaping heat

Trapped heat

The Sun heats the Earth

Atmosphere

Carbon dioxide in the atmosphere traps heat energy.

Coal

Coal contains energy from the Sun that was stored by plants that were alive when dinosaurs roamed the Earth. These plants were buried, then squashed and heated until they became coal.

Coal is dug up from the ground as a shiny, black rock.

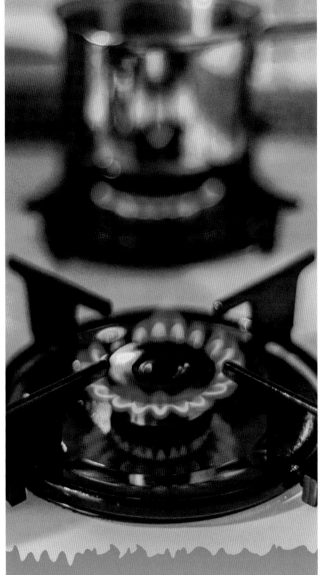

Oil

Oil is a sticky, black liquid that is often drilled out of the seabed by platforms called oil rigs. Oil is the remains of tiny ocean plants and animals that were buried beneath the ocean floor, and squashed and squeezed, turning them to oil.

Petrol is made from oil.

Natural gas

Natural gas is formed at the same time as oil, and is often found alongside it. It is also made from tiny plants and animals that were buried beneath the bottom of the ocean. We burn gas in hobs and ovens to cook our food.

Gas is often stored in tanks.

Renewable energy

We burn fossil fuels to release energy and make electricity, but fossil fuels are resources that will run out one day. Energy made using resources that won't run out is called renewable energy. There are many sources of renewable energy, for example, wind, sunlight, and the tides.

Solar
Light energy from the Sun is changed into electrical energy using solar panels. A different kind of panel can be used to heat water.

Hydroelectric
The potential energy of water trapped behind a dam can be made into electricity when the water is released and flows over a turbine.

Tidal
The tides are the rise and fall of the sea. This movement of water can push an underwater turbine in the same way wind pushes a wind turbine.

Saving energy

Energy is an important resource, so we're always trying to find ways to use less of it. You could switch off lights when you leave a room, and cycle to school instead of going by car.

Energy-saving light bulb

Biomass

Energy can be made by burning natural material or waste products, known as biomass. Wood and leftover crops can be used in this way.

Wood can be burnt to release energy. New trees can be planted to replace it.

Wind

Wind pushes the blades of a wind turbine around and a generator converts the kinetic energy into electricity.

Geothermal

Heat from inside the Earth can be used to make electricity. Water is piped deep below the ground, where it becomes steam. This steam can drive a turbine.

The water becomes steam and rises up, where it can spin a turbine.

Cold water is pumped below the Earth's surface.

Sparks of genius

Scientists have made brilliant discoveries about energy that have led to ways of making electricity, seeing deeper into space, and curing diseases. These energy pioneers helped us to understand how and why the Universe works the way it does.

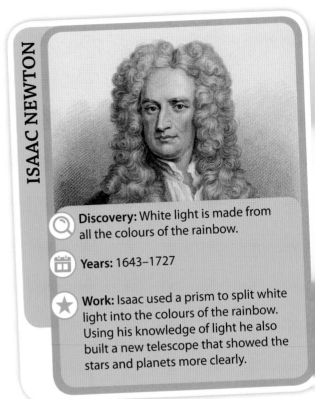

ISAAC NEWTON

Discovery: White light is made from all the colours of the rainbow.

Years: 1643–1727

Work: Isaac used a prism to split white light into the colours of the rainbow. Using his knowledge of light he also built a new telescope that showed the stars and planets more clearly.

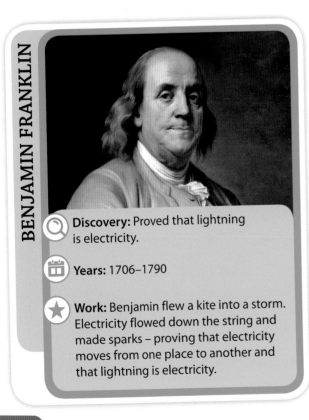

BENJAMIN FRANKLIN

Discovery: Proved that lightning is electricity.

Years: 1706–1790

Work: Benjamin flew a kite into a storm. Electricity flowed down the string and made sparks – proving that electricity moves from one place to another and that lightning is electricity.

CHRISTIAN DOPPLER

Discovery: How sound and light change when their source is moving.

Years: 1803–1853

Work: As a police car moves towards you the noise of the siren sounds higher, and as it moves away it sounds lower. This is called the Doppler effect. It also affects the colour of moving light.

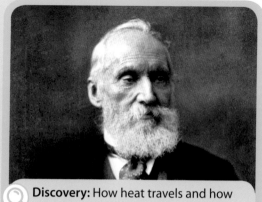

LORD KELVIN

Discovery: How heat travels and how we measure temperature.

Years: 1824–1907

Work: Lord Kelvin worked out the coldest temperature that a substance can be cooled to – a point known as absolute zero. He also explained how heat moves from hot to cold areas.

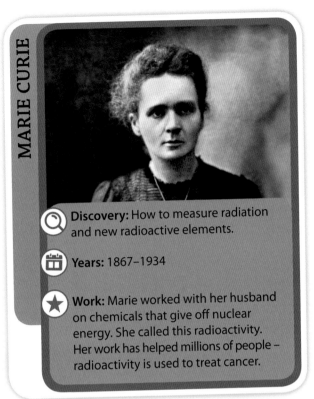

MARIE CURIE

Discovery: How to measure radiation and new radioactive elements.

Years: 1867–1934

Work: Marie worked with her husband on chemicals that give off nuclear energy. She called this radioactivity. Her work has helped millions of people – radioactivity is used to treat cancer.

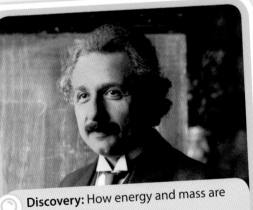

ALBERT EINSTEIN

Discovery: How energy and mass are related.

Years: 1879–1955

Work: Albert showed that all matter contains vast amounts of energy. His famous equation $E=mc^2$ shows how energy (E) can be calculated from mass (m), and the speed of light (c).

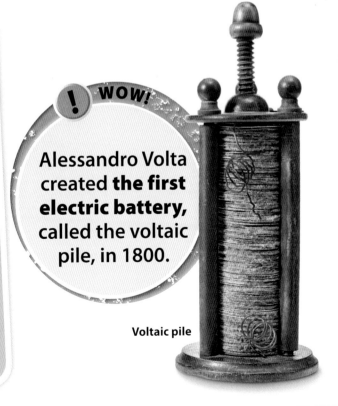

! WOW!

Alessandro Volta created **the first electric battery,** called the voltaic pile, in 1800.

Voltaic pile

Energy at home

All the energy that has ever existed began at the Big Bang, and has been powering everything that has happened since. This energy is all around us and in us – we use it every day in lots of different ways.

Listening to music

Electrical energy powers music systems. A speaker vibrates and sends out sound energy. Our ears detect that energy and we hear music.

! WOW!

Heating and cooling use up the most energy in a home.

Eating a meal

Food gives us energy to move and grow. The chemical energy in food is converted to movement and heat energy by our muscles.

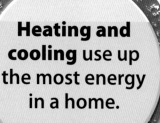

Switching on a light

When we switch on a light, electrical energy flows through a circuit and into the light bulb. The light glows, and gives out light and heat energy.

Cycling

When you cycle, you use the chemical energy in your muscles to move your legs and push the pedals down. The pedals move the wheels and off you go!

Cooking

Electrical energy is used to power electric ovens, which release heat energy to heat up and cook food.

Interview with...

We put some questions to Dr Canan Dagdeviren, an assistant professor at the Massachusetts Institute of Technology (MIT). She works on devices that create electricity from movement.

Q: We know it is something to do with energy, but what do you actually do?

A: I create flexible devices that look like stickers and change energy from the natural movements of internal organs, such as the beating of a heart or the expanding and deflating of a lung, into electricity. Enough electricity can be made to power a machine such as a pacemaker, which is put inside the body to regulate irregular heartbeats.

Q: What made you decide to become a scientist?

A: When I was a child in the early 1990s, I learned that my grandfather had died of heart failure at just 28 years old. I made a promise to myself to do something to tackle the condition that struck my grandfather.

Q: What are these devices called?

A: They are called piezoelectric devices, and they create a small electric charge as they bend. Stuck to the lungs, for example, the device changes shape as a person breathes in and out, delivering a steady current.

Q: What are the uses of these devices?

A: They could be used anywhere we need electrical energy. Inside the body, they can power medical machines, so you don't have to change the machine's batteries.

Q: What sort of equipment do you use?

A: I use drawing programs on a computer to design the structure of my device. I also use microscopes to see the parts of the device itself, which may be very small.

Q: What are the best and worst parts of your job?

A: The best part is that I can make my dreams come true. There is no worst part. If you really love to do something, you'll experience no worst at all.

Q: What do you think the future of making energy will be?

A: Little, tiny devices will be a part of your clothing, and whenever you do your daily activities, you'll be generating electrical power. Free energy!

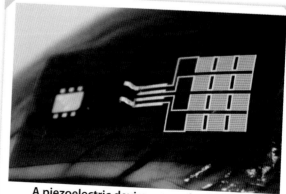

A piezoelectric device can make electricity using the movement of internal organs.

Canan working on a
piezoelectric device
in her lab.

Future of energy

Scientists are always coming up with new ideas for ways to use energy and make electricity. Some of these ideas might sound far-fetched or strange, but many of the great energy discoveries from the past seemed strange at the time, too!

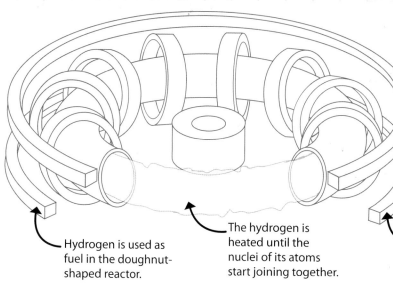

Fusion reactor

Lots of energy is released by the Sun when the nuclei of its atoms join together, in the process called nuclear fusion. Scientists are working on machines called fusion reactors that try and recreate this, to make huge amounts of electricity.

Hydrogen is used as fuel in the doughnut-shaped reactor.

The hydrogen is heated until the nuclei of its atoms start joining together.

The superhot hydrogen, called plasma, is held in place with magnets.

People power

"Piezoelectric" devices can make electricity out of movement. In a train station in Japan, pedestrians could walk on tiles that created electric currents when they were squashed. The electricity they created powered Christmas lights.

Stepping on these panels creates electricity.

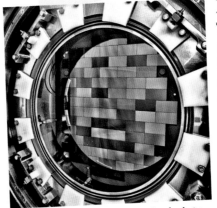

The Dark Energy Camera looks into space, searching for evidence of dark energy.

Dark energy

The Universe is always expanding, but faster than scientists expect. One explanation is that there is a type of energy called "dark energy" making it go faster. If it exists, this mysterious energy could maybe be used to make power for planet Earth.

Magma power

Geothermal power stations generate electricity using water that is pumped underground, where temperatures reach around 300°C (572°F). However, engineers are working on drilling deeper down, towards a magma chamber, where the water could be heated to 1,000°C (1,832°F)!

Dyson sphere

A Dyson sphere is a Solar-System-sized container to surround a star and capture all the energy it gives out. This futuristic idea involves putting a solid shell, or many smaller devices, around a star to collect all its heat and light energy. We don't have the technology to do it yet though!

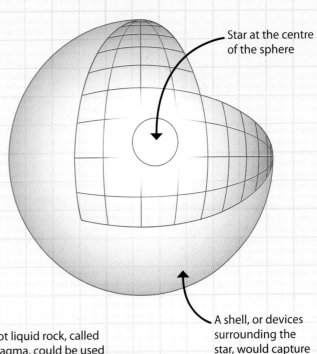

Star at the centre of the sphere

A shell, or devices surrounding the star, would capture its energy.

Hot liquid rock, called magma, could be used to heat water, to make lots of electricity.

Energy facts and figures

Energy is amazing. It's everywhere and everything works because it exists. Here are some energy facts and figures to impress your friends with!

A **BROWN BEAR** can gain **180 KG** (400 lb) of fat a year, so it has enough energy to survive its winter hibernation.

LIGHT IS ALMOST 900,000 TIMES FASTER THAN SOUND.

That's why you see lightning before you hear the thunder it creates.

80%

The amount of electricity in a light bulb that is lost as heat.

180 dB

The volume in decibels heard 160 km (100 miles) away when the volcano Krakatoa erupted in 1883.

The USA makes around a third of the world's nuclear power.

THE WORLD'S MOST POWERFUL **WIND TURBINE** HAS **BLADES LONGER** THAN **NINE BUSES**.

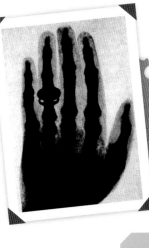

William Röntgen discovered X-rays in **1895**.

Some **power stations create electricity** by burning **chicken manure**.

8.6 million

The number of lightning strikes on Earth every day.

−219°C

(−362°F). The temperature oxygen must drop below for it to become a solid.

# Glossary

Here are the meanings of some words that are useful for you to know when learning about energy.

atmosphere Thick layer of gases around the Earth that trap the Sun's heat energy and protect the planet from the Sun's dangerous rays

atom Tiny particles that everything is made from. They are the smallest part of something that can take part in a chemical reaction

boil When a liquid is heated to a temperature at which it bubbles and turns into a gas

bond Join between two or more atoms which stores chemical energy

carbon dioxide Gas found in the atmosphere produced by living things, volcanoes, and by burning fossil fuels

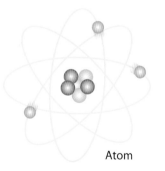
Atom

chemical Substance made by a reaction between particles such as atoms

chemical energy Energy stored inside chemicals in their bonds, which can be released or produced in a chemical reaction

circuit Loop that an electric current travels around

condensation When a gas cools and forms a liquid. Also the name of the water droplets on cold windows, formed by condensation

conductor Substance that allows heat or electricity to pass through it easily

echo Sound that has bounced off a surface and travels back in the direction it started from

electrical appliance Item such as a television, fridge, or oven, that needs electricity to work

electrical energy Energy that tiny particles called electrons carry as they flow in an electric current

electromagnetic spectrum Range of electric and magnetic waves that carry different amounts of energy, including visible light, X-rays, radio waves, and ultraviolet light

electron Tiny, negatively charged particle that moves around the nucleus of an atom

energy What makes things happen. It is found in different forms, including heat, light, movement, sound, and electricity.

evaporation When a liquid is heated and changes into a gas or vapour

fat Chemical material in the body used to store energy

force Push or pull that causes things to start moving, move faster, change direction, slow down, or stop moving

fossil fuels Fuels made from animals and plants that died millions of years ago, for example, coal

fuel Substance that releases heat when it is burned, often to make electricity

gas State of matter with no fixed shape, such as air, that expands to fill any space it is in

generator Machine that creates electrical energy using movement and magnets

gravity Force that pulls objects towards each other

heat Type of energy that warms things

insulator Substance that does not allow heat or electricity to pass easily through it

kinetic energy Movement energy

light Part of the electromagnetic spectrum that humans can see

Light bulb

liquid State of matter that flows and takes the shape of any container that holds it

magnetic energy Energy of a magnetic field

magnetic field Force field surrounding a magnet, in which magnetic materials can be attracted or repelled

matter Stuff that all things are made of

melting When a solid is heated and becomes a liquid

nuclear energy Energy released when the nuclei at the centre of atoms break apart or join together

nucleus Central area of an atom containing the positively charged protons, and neutrons, which have no charge

oxygen Gas found in the atmosphere produced by plants and some bacteria

particle Extremely small part of a solid, liquid, or gas

photosynthesis Process that green plants use to make food

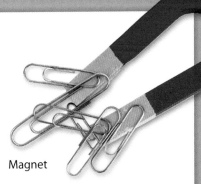
Magnet

potential energy Energy stored in things, ready to be used to do something

pressure Force of gases and liquids when they are squashed and contained

renewable energy Sources of energy other than fossil fuels, that are used to generate electricity. Renewables will never run out, unlike fossil fuels

shadow Dark area formed when light rays are blocked by a solid object

solid State of matter that holds its shape

sound Form of energy that is produced when objects vibrate, and can be heard

turbine Fanlike set of blades that are turned by wind, water, or steam

vibration Back and forth movement. Vibrations produce sound

Index

Acknowledgements

The publisher would like to thank the following people for their assistance in the preparation of this book: Lucy Sims, Emma Hobson, and Yamini Panwar for design assistance, Marie Greenwood and Roohi Sehgal for editorial assistance, Dan Crisp for illustrations, Polly Goodman for proofreading, and Helen Peters for compiling the index. The publishers would also like to thank Dr Canan Dagdeviren for the "Interview with…" interview.

The publisher would like to thank the following for their kind permission to reproduce their photographs:

(Key: a-above; b-below/bottom; c-centre; f-far; l-left; r-right; t-top)

2 123RF.com: Pongsak Deethongngam (cb). Alamy Stock Photo: D. Hurst (bl). 3 Dorling Kindersley: Arran Lewis / NASA (bc); Whipple Museum of History of Science, Cambridge (bl). NASA: (br). 4-5 NASA. 4 Dreamstime.com: Juliengrondin (br). iStockphoto.com: Chaluk (bl). 5 123RF.com: Andrey Alyukhin (tr); Soleg (bc). iStockphoto.com: Shapecharge (br). 6 Dorling Kindersley: Arran Lewis / NASA (bl). 7 NASA: NASA / SDO (cla). 8 123RF.com: Chris Pole (cra). iStockphoto.com: Lchumpitaz (br). NASA: (clb). 9 Dorling Kindersley: Stephen Oliver (cla). 10 Alamy Stock Photo: Wavebreak Media ltd. 11 Alamy Stock Photo: Hero Images Inc. 12-13 Getty Images: Mint Images - Frans Lanting. 13 iStockphoto.com: RichVintage (cb). 14 Dorling Kindersley: Dan Crisp (bl). iStockphoto.com: Dvoinik (cr). 15 Alamy Stock Photo: Erik Reis (crb). 16 Alamy Stock Photo: D. Hurst (cr). Dreamstime.com: Carolyn Franks (br). 17 123RF.com: Evgeniy Zakharov (cl). Getty Images: Hulton Deutsch (tc). 18 123RF.com: ktsdesign (c). SuperStock: Minden Pictures (br). 19 iStockphoto.com: Watcherff (bc). SuperStock: NaturePL (br). 20 NASA: NASA / DOE / Fermi LAT Collaboration (clb). 21 123RF.com: Suwat Phatthanawadee (clb). Alamy Stock Photo: Cultura RM (br). Dorling Kindersley: Dan Crisp (tl). Fotolia: Natallia Yaumenenka / eAlisa (cr). Science Photo Library: Cordelia Molloy (tl/marsh). 22-23 Getty Images: Ian Mcallister (c). 23 123RF.com: evrenkalinbacak (clb). 24-25 Alamy Stock Photo: Bruce Beck. 25 Alamy Stock Photo: Jeff Rotman (crb). 26-27 Alamy Stock Photo: Blickwinkel. 28 Alamy Stock Photo: Agencja Fotograficzna Caro (cl); Agencja Fotograficzna Caro (cr). 29 123RF.com: Viktoriya Kuzmenkova (cla). Alamy Stock Photo: Agencja Fotograficzna Caro (cl). Dreamstime.com: Artem Gorohov / Agorohov (cr). iStockphoto.com: LOU63 (cra). 30-31 123RF.com: Todsaporn Bunmuen / addtodsaporn (c). 30 Dreamstime.com: Pablo Hidalgo / Pxhidalgo (crb). 31 Dreamstime.com: Andrey Bayda (crb). Science Photo Library: Edward Kinsman (clb). 33 Dreamstime.com: Vladimir Seliverstov / Vladsilver (cla). 34-35 Getty Images: Jeremy Walker. 35 123RF.com: Anzemulec (r). Dorling Kindersley: Stephen Oliver (tc). 36-37 Getty Images: Barcroft (c). 37 123RF.com: Yutakapong chuynugul (cr). 39 Dorling Kindersley: Positiveflash (br). 40-41 Dorling Kindersley: Stephen Oliver (circuit). Dreamstime.com: Hywit Dimyadi / Photosoup. 43 123RF.com: Iakov Filimonov / jackf (cra). 45 123RF.com: byrdyak (tr); Alexey Koldunov (br). 46 123RF.com: Pongsak Deethongngam (br). Getty Images: ewg3D (tr). 47 123RF.com: Jezper (tl); Phive2015 (bc); Oleksandr Marynchenko (br). iStockphoto.com: DorukTR (tr). 49 123RF.com: Teerawut Masawat / jannoon028 (tc). 50 Alamy Stock Photo: Paul Fearn (crb); Wim Wiskerke (clb). Dreamstime.com: Georgios Kollidas / Georgios (tr). 51 Alamy Stock Photo: GL Archive (clb); Pictorial Press Ltd (tl); The Print Collector (tr). Dorling Kindersley: Whipple Museum of History of Science, Cambridge (br). 52 iStockphoto.com: RuslanDashinsky (cb); ShikharBhattarai (c). 53 123RF.com: Aleksandar Mijatovic (tc). iStockphoto.com: Icealien (bl); Waldru (crb). 54-55 Canan Dagdeviren: (All). 56 Dreamstime.com: Andreykuzmin (t). Getty Images: YOSHIKAZU TSUNO (br). 57 Science Photo Library: Fermi National Accelerator Laboratory / US DEPARTMENT OF ENERGY (tc). 58 Alamy Stock Photo: Westend61 GmbH (br). Dreamstime.com: Daria Rybakova / Podarenka (r). 59 123RF.com: Alexeysmirnov (br). Alamy Stock Photo: INTERFOTO (cl). Dorling Kindersley: Barleylands Farm Museum and Animal Centre, Billericay (cr). 61 123RF.com: Teerawut Masawat / jannoon028 (br). 62 Fotolia: apttone (tl). 64 NASA

Endpaper images: Front: 123RF.com: Lubos Chlubny c (coal), Alfio Scisetti cla; Alamy Stock Photo: Tawatchai Khid-arn c; Dreamstime.com: Dimitar Marinov / Oorka cr, Oxfordsquare fcrb, Radha Karuppannan / Radhuvenki bc; Back: 123RF.com: Daniel Prudek cb; Alamy Stock Photo: Lindsay Constable cra, Dmitri Maruta bc (Tesla); Dorling Kindersley: The Science Museum tc The Science Museum, London bc;

Cover images: Front: 123RF.com: Didier Kobi cb/ (mic); Dorling Kindersley: Arran Lewis / NASA cr; Dreamstime.com: Dimitar Marinov / Oorka b, Radha Karuppannan / Radhuvenki ca; Fotolia: Valdis Torms c; Getty Images: artpartner-images cb, Dan McCoy - Rainbow l; Back: 123RF.com: Soleg cr; Front Flap: 123RF.com: Pongsak Deethongngam tc, Oleksandr Marynchenko cra/1, Teerawut Masawat / jannoon028 fcrb, Phive2015 br/1; Alamy Stock Photo: D. Hurst clb; Dreamstime.com: Stephen Sweet / Cornishman c; iStockphoto.com: LOU63 cr, Ozandogan bl; Back Flap: 123RF.com: Audrius Merfeldas tl; Dorling Kindersley: Wardrobe Museum, Salisbury br; iStockphoto.com: naumoid c

All other images © Dorling Kindersley
For further information see:
www.dkimages.com

My Findout facts:

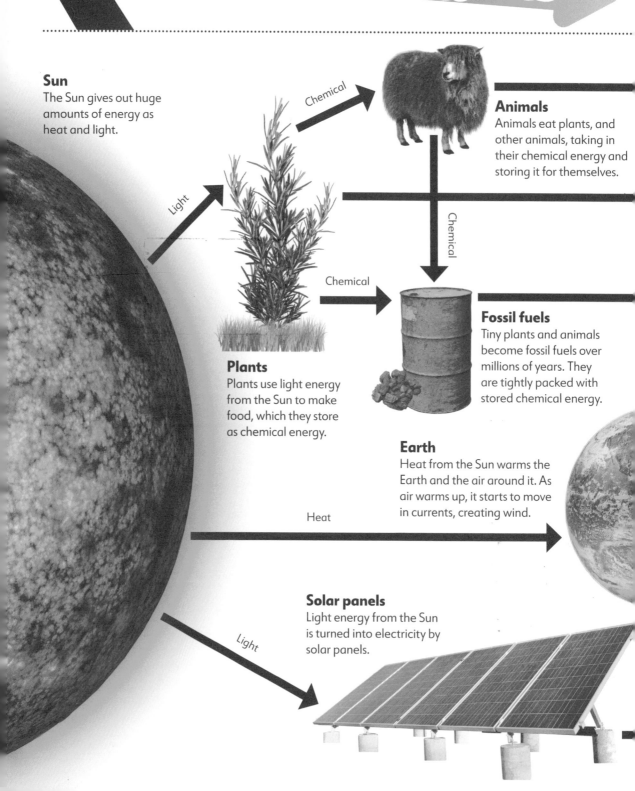

Sun
The Sun gives out huge amounts of energy as heat and light.

Chemical

Animals
Animals eat plants, and other animals, taking in their chemical energy and storing it for themselves.

Light

Chemical

Chemical

Plants
Plants use light energy from the Sun to make food, which they store as chemical energy.

Fossil fuels
Tiny plants and animals become fossil fuels over millions of years. They are tightly packed with stored chemical energy.

Earth
Heat from the Sun warms the Earth and the air around it. As air warms up, it starts to move in currents, creating wind.

Heat

Solar panels
Light energy from the Sun is turned into electricity by solar panels.

Light